D0819825

2

$200
A+L

ULTRA 3-D®

FINE ART PRINT BOOK

Front Line Art Publishing
Montage Publications Division
San Diego, California USA

•

Quarto Publishing
London, England

ULTRA 3-D® copyright © 1994 by Montage Publications. All rights reserved. No part of this book may be used or reproduced in any manner whatsoever without written permission except in the case of reprints in the context of reviews. For information, write Montage Publications, 9808 Waples Street, San Diego, California USA 92121.

ISBN: I -56714-025-4

First Printing, July 1994

3-D Artists :
We are currently preparing a new 3-D book
please send submissions to:
MONTAGE PUBLICATIONS
3-D ART SUBMISSIONS
9808 WAPLES STREET
SAN DIEGO, CALIFORNIA 92121 USA
Include self-addressed stamped envelope.

FOREWORD

Welcome to the beginning of a new and challenging art form. Although 3-D images and stereograms have been around for decades in many different forms, we have now entered the age where we need only our eyes and minds to create amazing illusions of depth. This new art form is so visually stimulating, you will find yourself actually reaching out to touch the images that seem so real, just beyond the printed page.

From the very first page of ULTRA 3-D®, you realize that you are in for a fantastic ride. Through a wonderous mix of art and science, these amazing images will transport you to 24 different worlds, each with incredible detail and depth. As you stare at the fields of colors, lines and patterns, they will begin to swirl, move and separate when suddenly...

You are gliding along the bottom of the sea with playful dolphins and majestic whales.

You are traveling to the outer-most reaches of the galaxy where sleek starfighters roar.

You are roaming the tropical rainforests encountering the splendid variety of its inhabitants.

You are soaring the skies on the wings of a mythical horse, the landscapes below endless and inspiring.

ULTRA 3-D® has been created for everyone. An innovative and creative challenge to the most sophisticated viewer, and a relaxing experience for those who wish to enjoy a unique, new art form.

Enjoy

ULTRA 3-D® art by Johnny Ray Barnes Jr., Marty Engle, Francois Guerin, Ali Vafaei, Lee Ellingson
Cover design by Marty Engle

ULTRA 3-D®

When viewed properly, stereograms and 3-D art prints can spring to mind many pleasant surprises. Remember to relax (both the mind and eye) and have patience. There are several ways to view the prints depending on size and format.

GENERAL VIEWING INSTRUCTIONS:

View at eye level. Stand at a medium distance from the image (2 to 4 ft.). Concentrate on your reflection or the reflection of light on the image. Stare THROUGH the picture as if you were looking at something a distance BEHIND the image. Keep focused on one area of the image. Depending on the eyesight of the viewer, different lengths of time may be required for the image to become clear. CONTINUE STARING as the image will appear. When the pattern begins to move or shift, the image is about to form. If you have trouble seeing the image, try standing with your nose just touching the print. Stare at the print at this distance and keep your eyes fixed at that position while slowly backing away from the print. Continue backing away until the image begins to form. Be patient as it takes some practice.

IF THE PRINT IS BEHIND GLASS:

• Start by looking at your own reflection in the glass cover.
• Then look beyond the reflection into the back of the picture, as if you are looking through a window.
• Keep staring through the picture. Once you see the image the first time, it becomes easier to see it again.

IF THE PRINT HAS NO REFLECTIVE SURFACE:

• Hold the print just at the end of your nose. Let your eyes relax and let the picture be out of focus. Just keep staring through the picture, not at it.
• Slowly move the print away from your face, continuing to look through the picture. Stop at a comfortable reading distance.
• When you start to see an image come into focus, keep staring through it.

AN ALTERNATIVE TECHNIQUE:

• Focus on an object in the distance.
• Maintaining that focal point, insert the print between your eyes and the distant object.
• The print will be blurry. Keep your eyes focused exactly as they are, staring blankly, without actually "looking" at anything.
• Move the print slowly forward and backward.
• When the print reaches the right position, the three-dimensional image will come into focus.

MYTHICAL FLIGHT

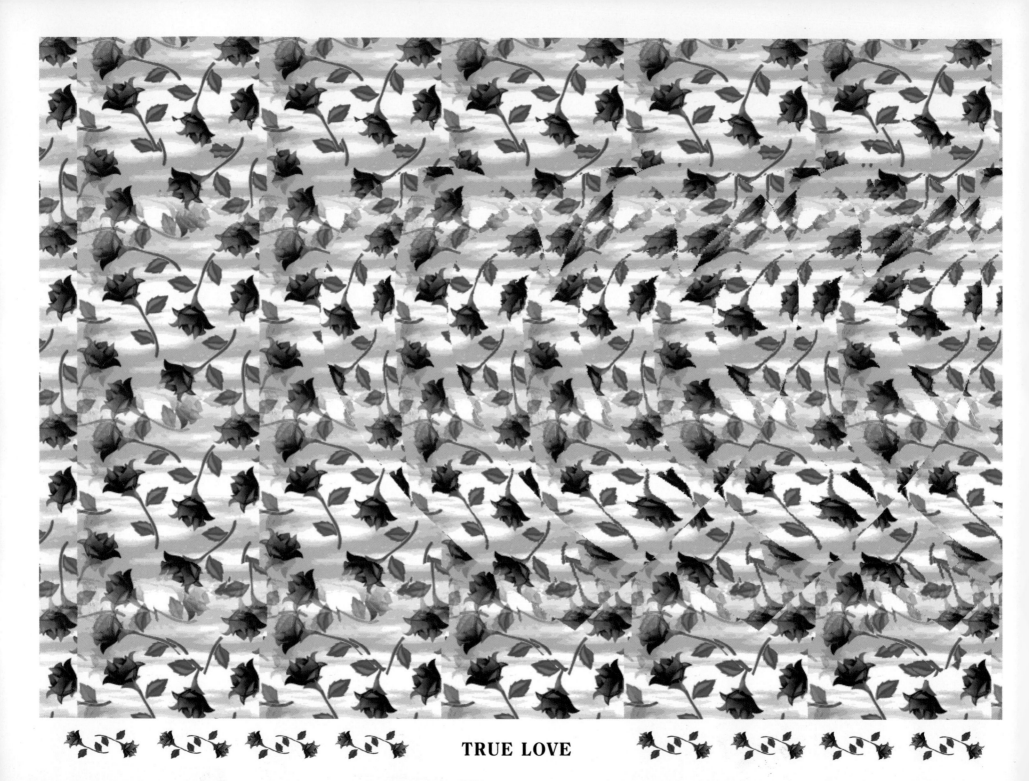

TRUE LOVE

PREDATORS OF THE DEEP

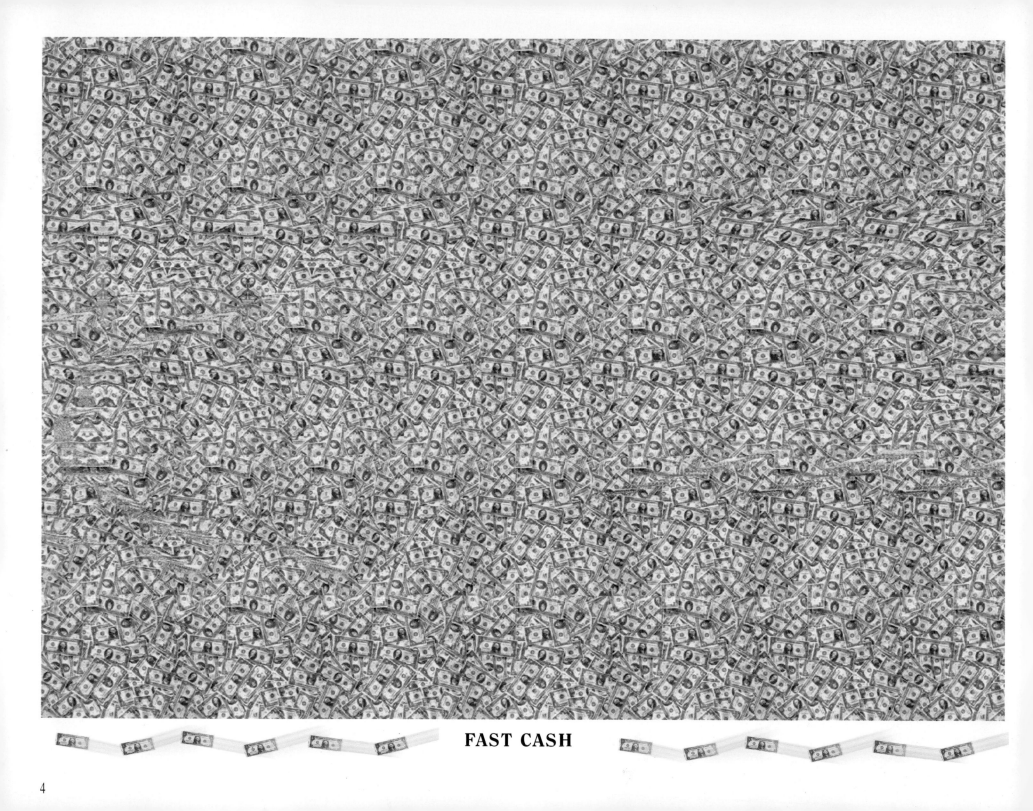

FAST CASH

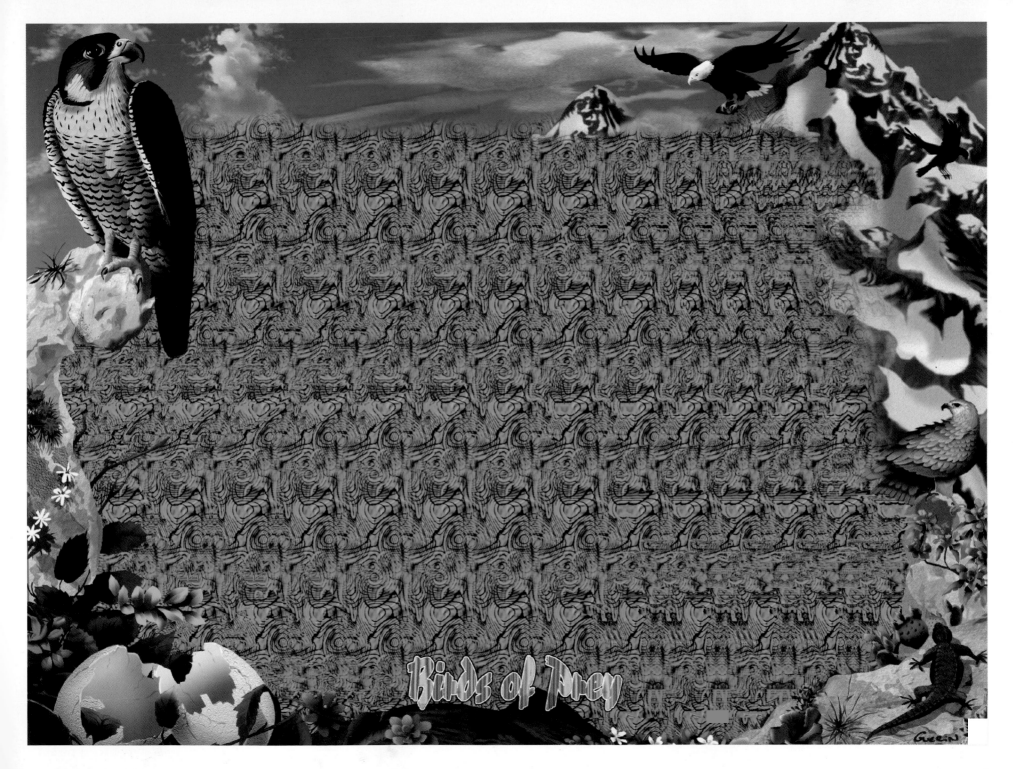

Birds of Prey

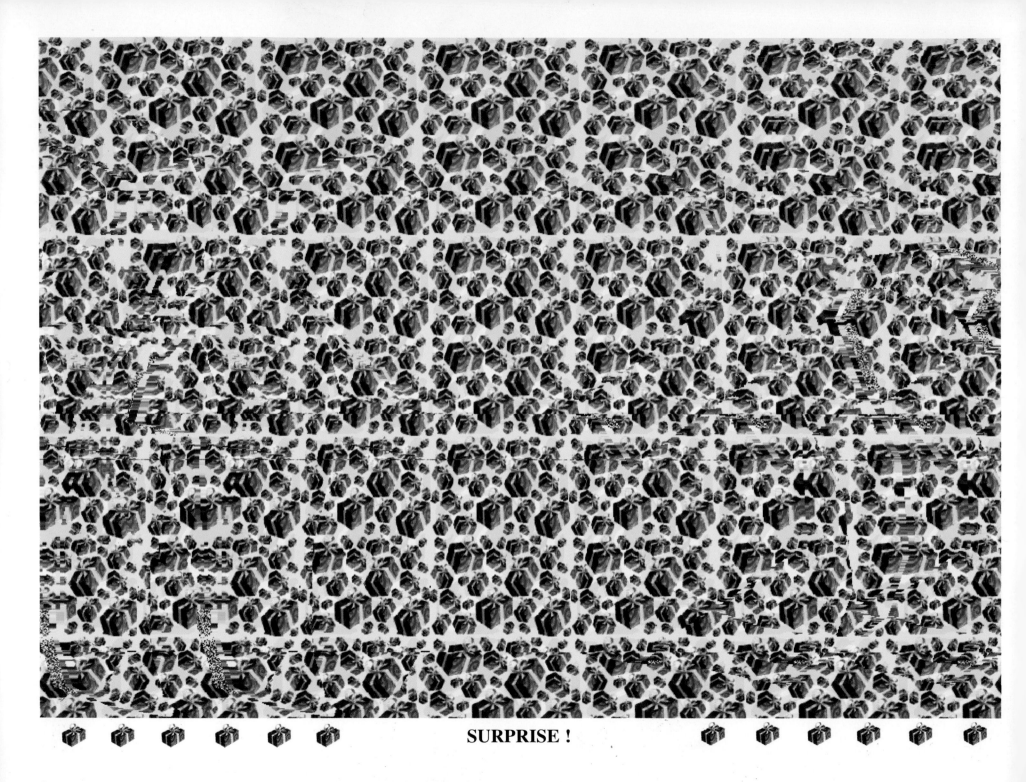

SURPRISE !

NIGHT HOWL

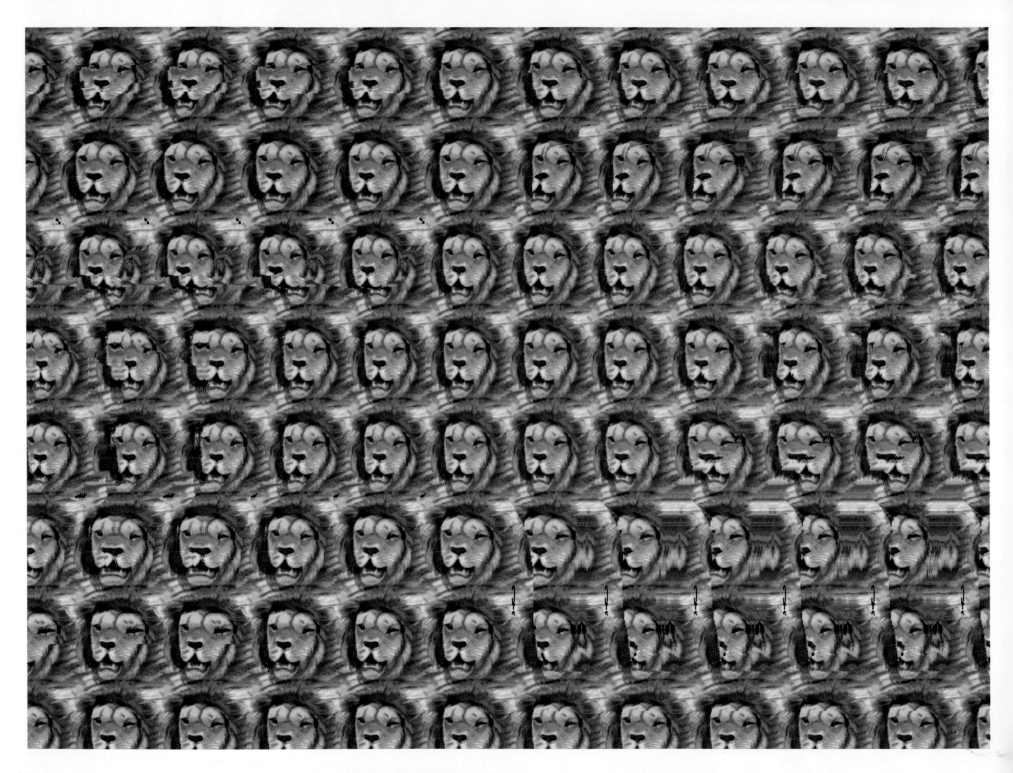

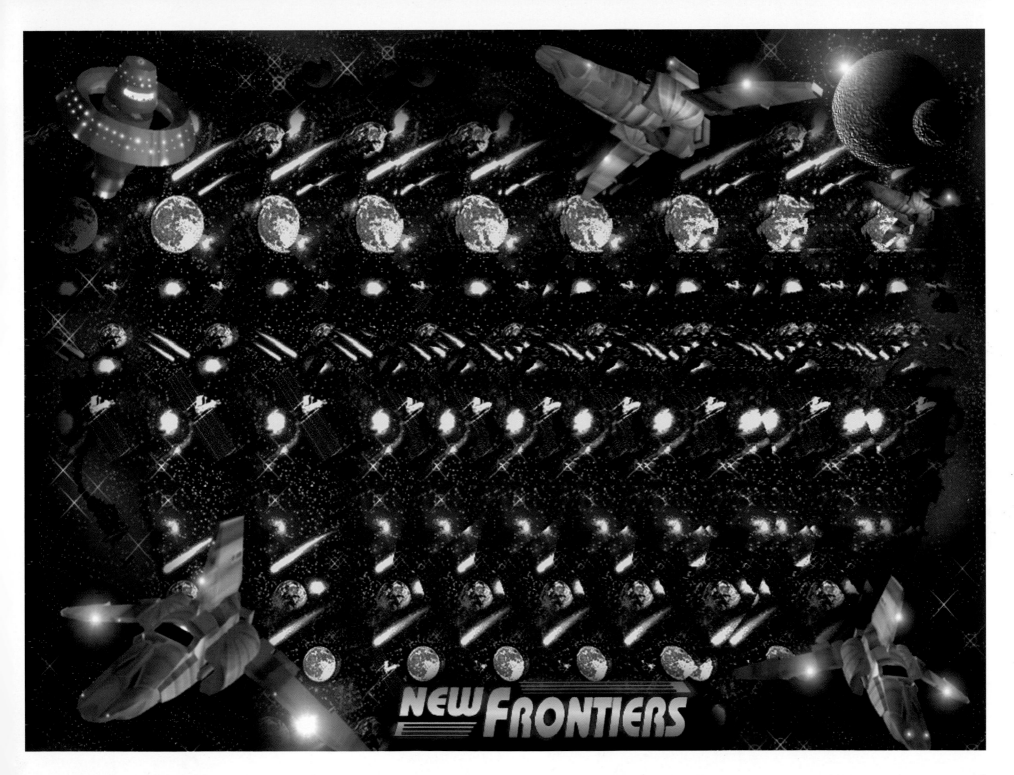

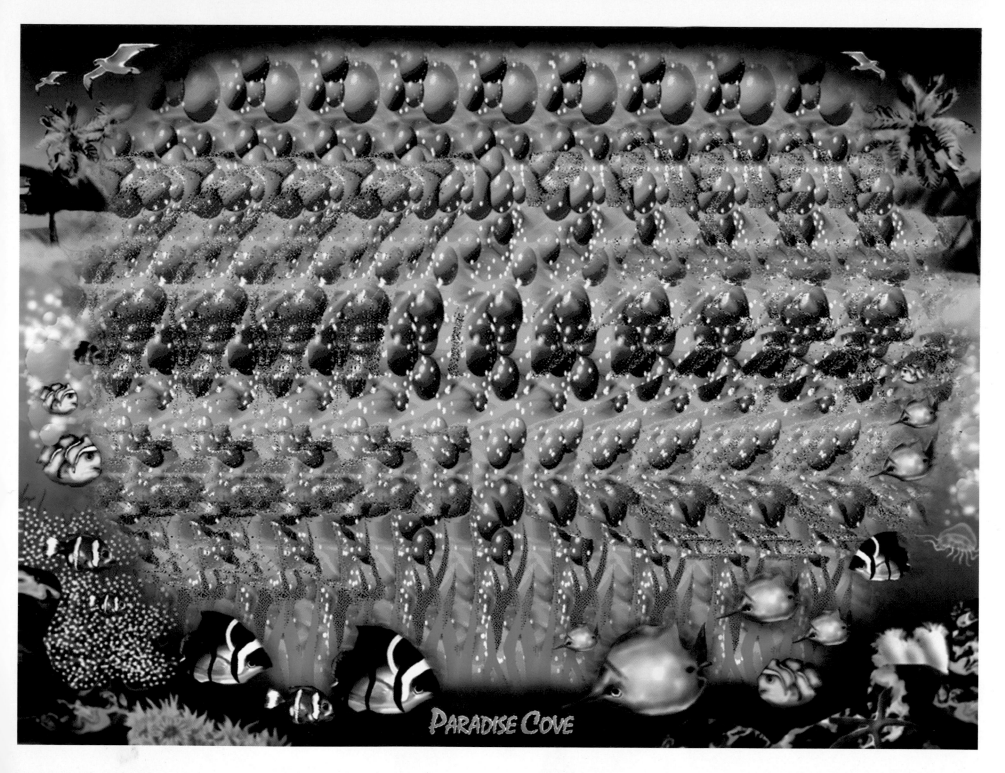

PARADISE COVE

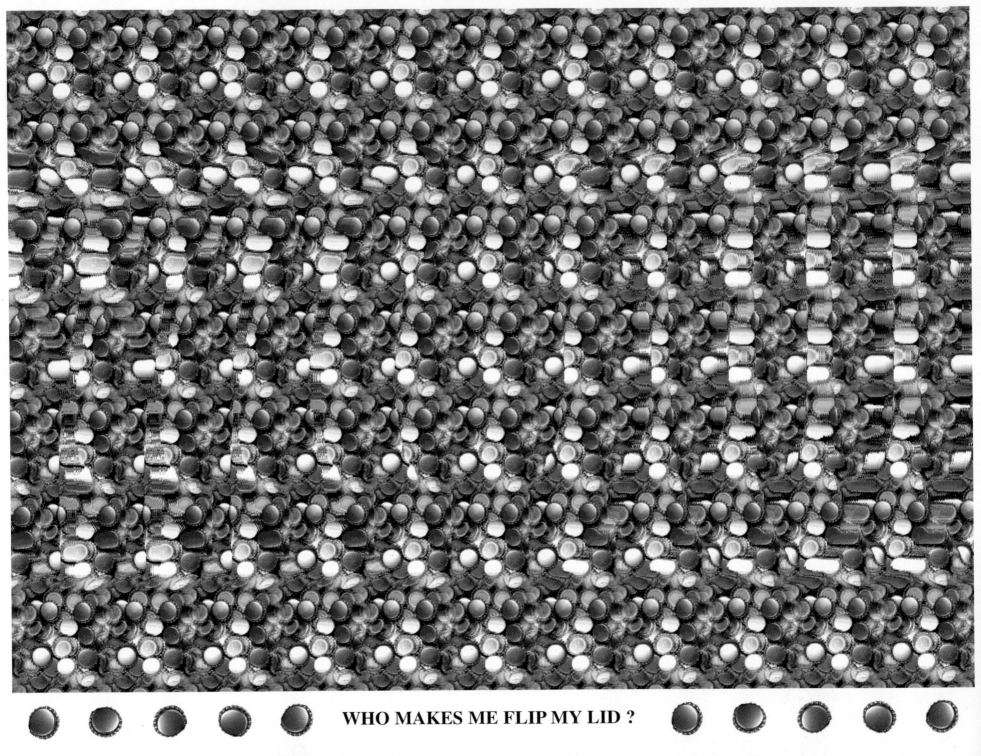

WHO MAKES ME FLIP MY LID ?

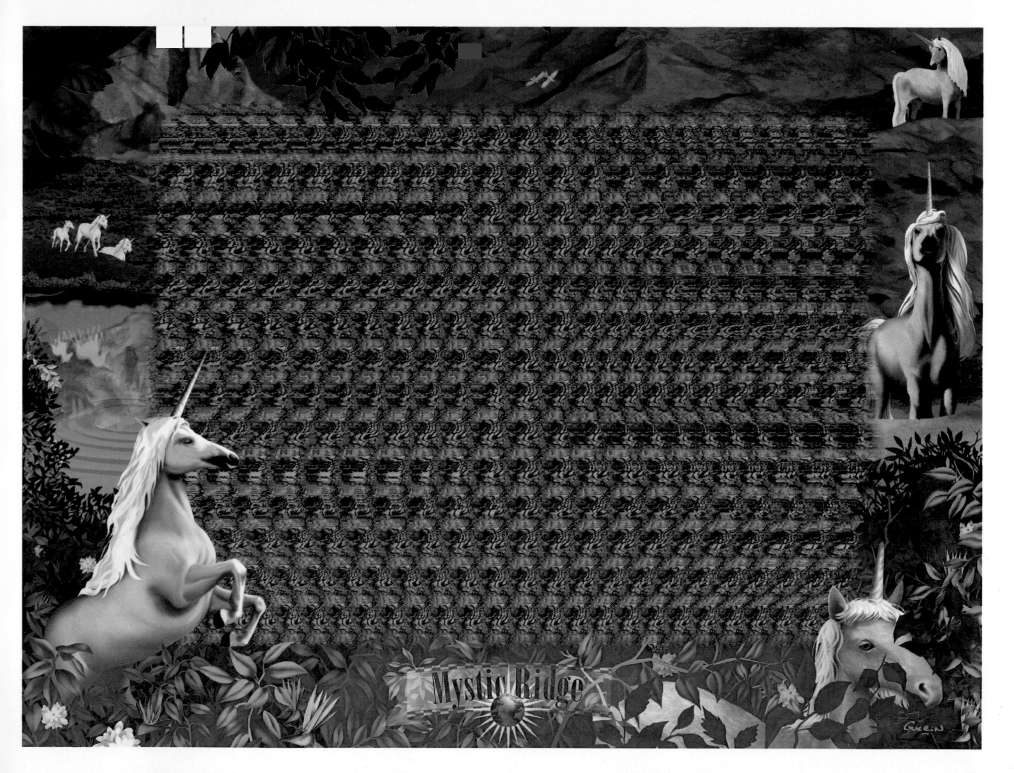

Mystic Ridge

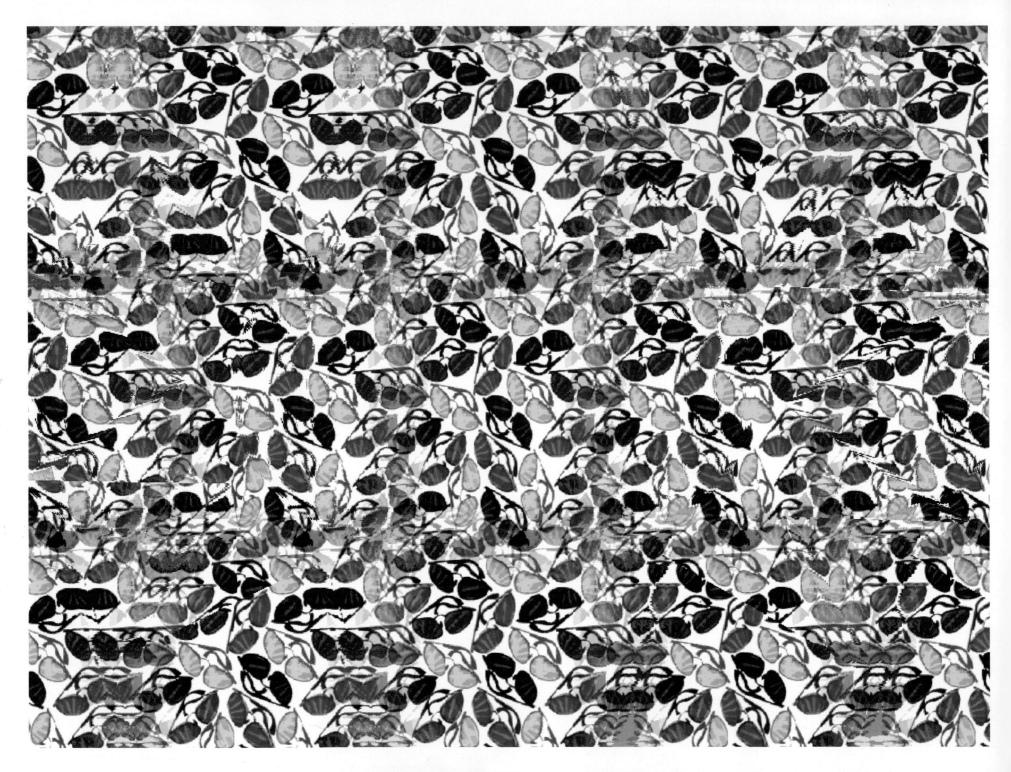

Hidden
RAINFOREST

15

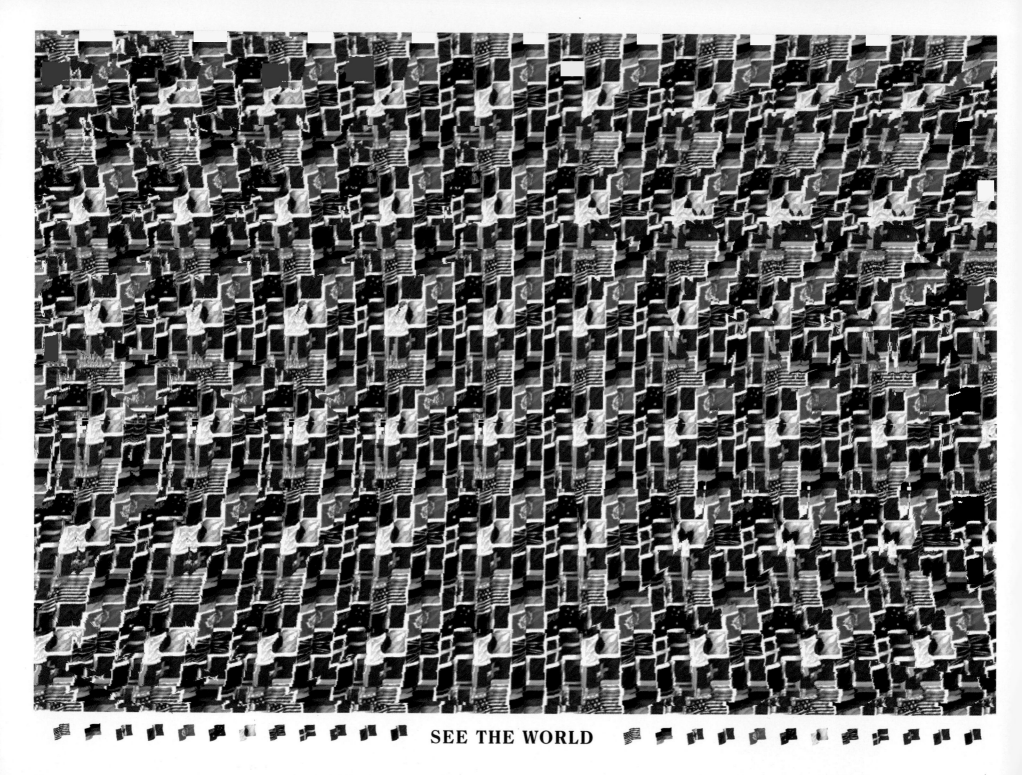

SEE THE WORLD

16

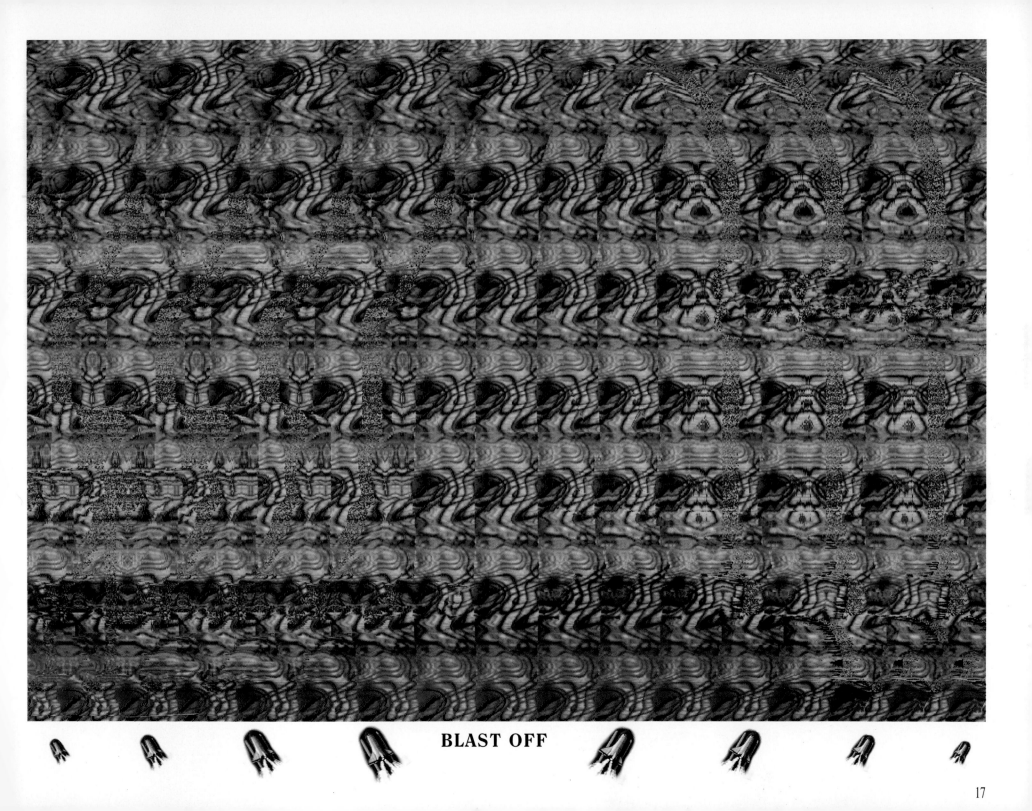

BLAST OFF

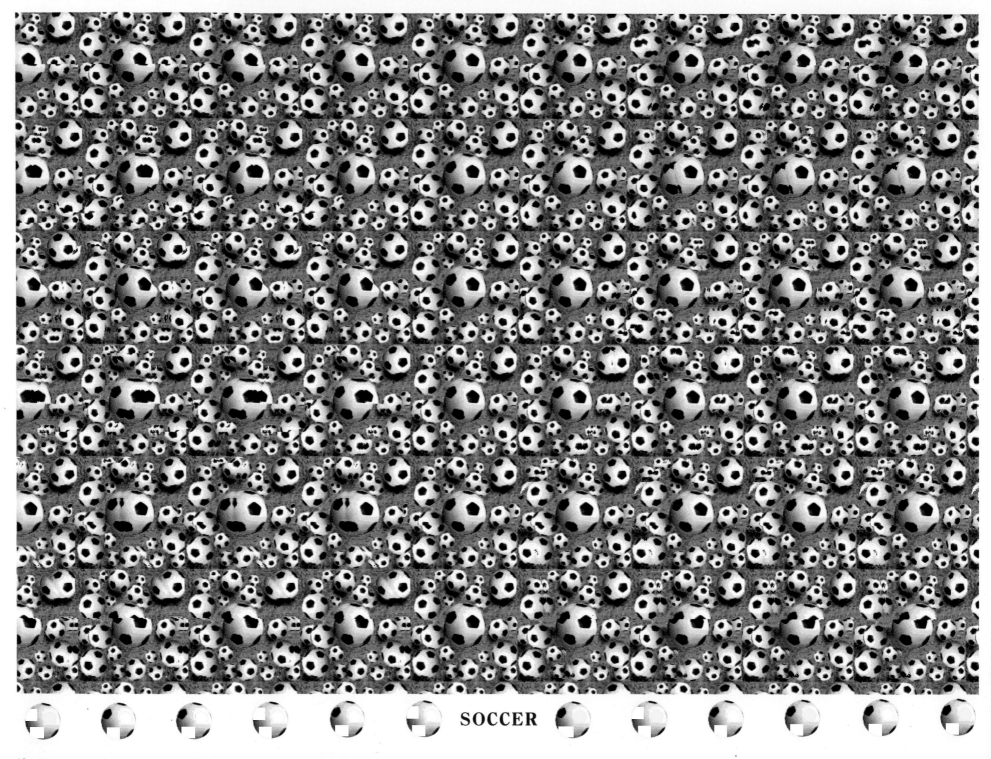

SOCCER

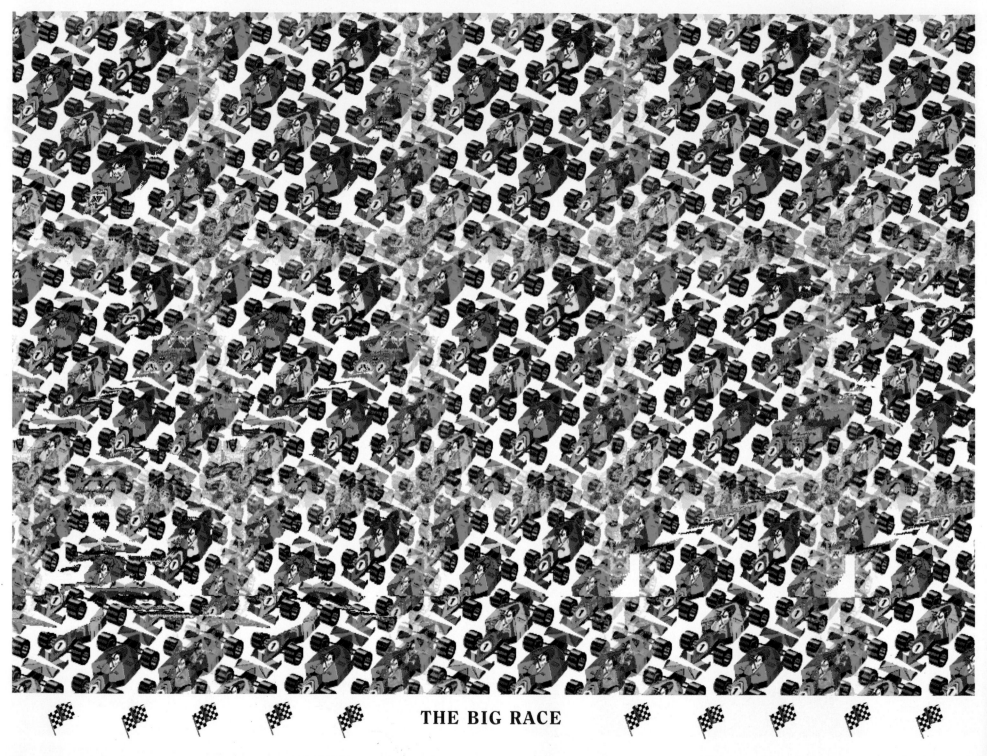

THE BIG RACE

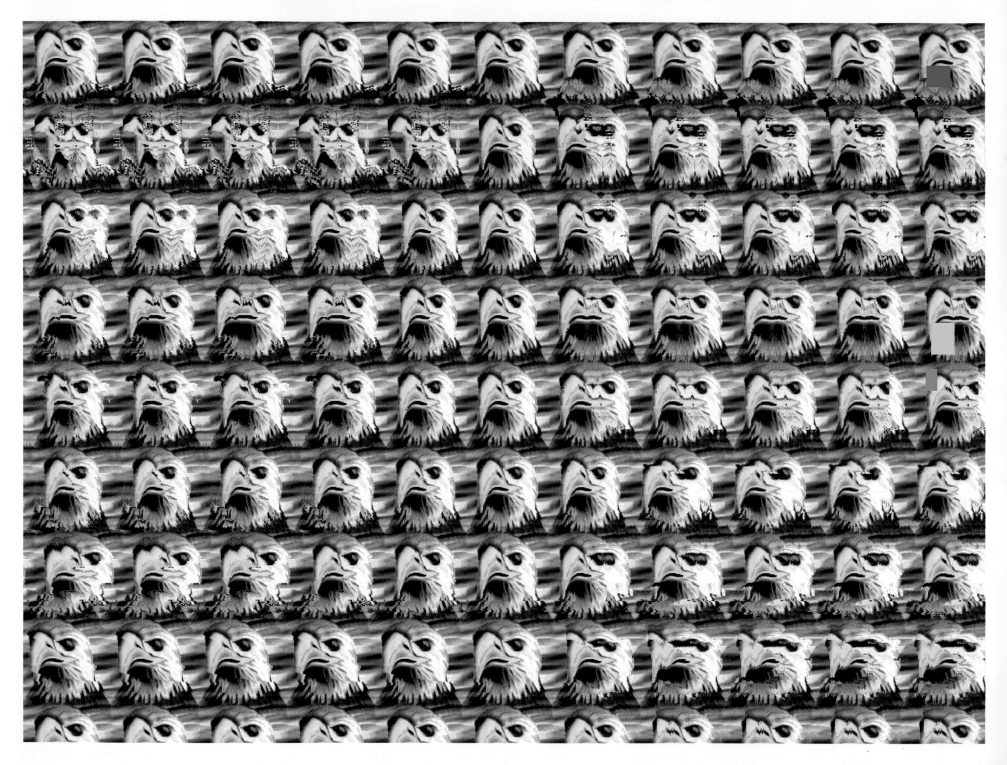

TYRANNOSAURUS REX

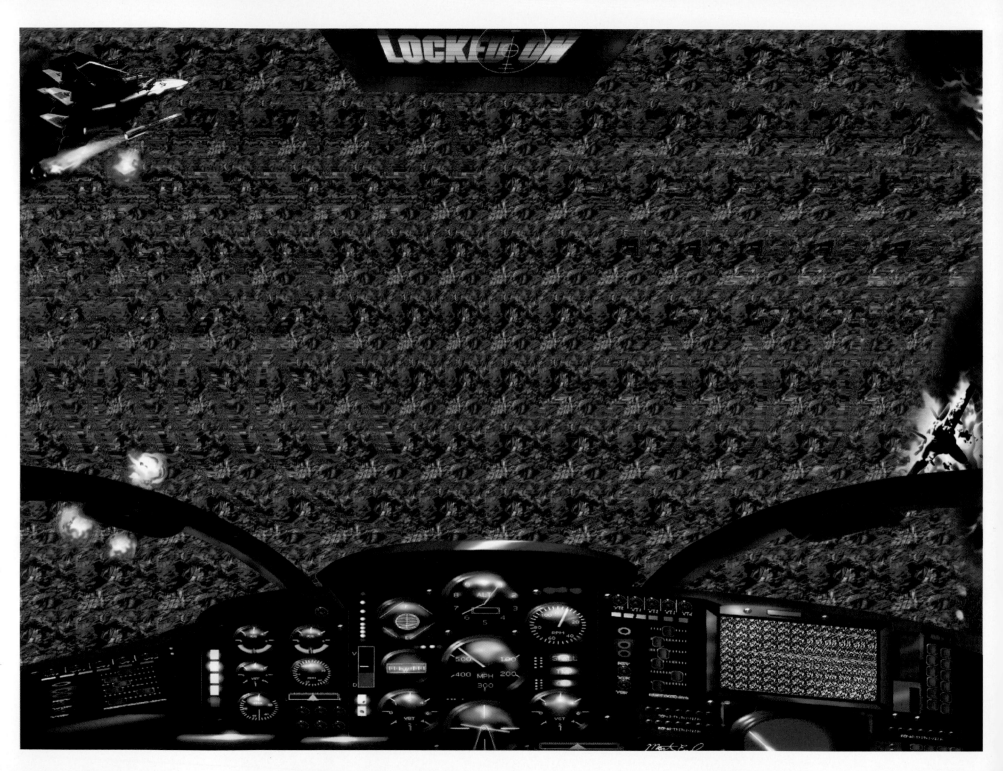

ULTRA 3-D
HIDDEN IMAGES

MYTHICAL FLIGHT

1

TRUE LOVE

2

PREDATORS OF THE DEEP

3

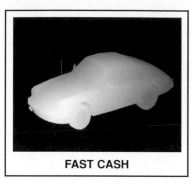

FAST CASH

4

BIRDS OF PREY

5

SURPRISE!

6

NIGHT HOWL

7

LION

8

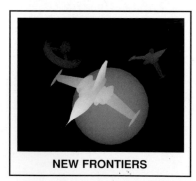

NEW FRONTIERS

9

KISS ME

10

PARADISE COVE

11

WHO MAKES ME FLIP MY LID?

12

ULTRA 3-D

HIDDEN IMAGES

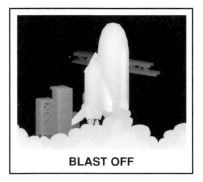

MYSTIC RIDGE

13

SUNGLASSES

14

HIDDEN RAINFOREST

15

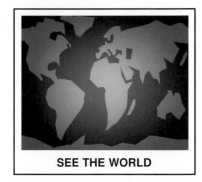

SEE THE WORLD

16

BLAST OFF

17

SOCCER

18

ATLANTIS

19

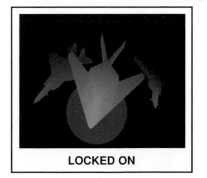

THE BIG RACE

20

EAGLE

22

TYRANNASAURUS REX

23

LOCKED ON

24

CRYSTAL REEF

25